My Graduation

My Graduation

Maria Morales

iUniverse, Inc.
Bloomington

My Graduation

iUniverse books may be ordered through booksellers or by contacting:

iUniverse
1663 Liberty Drive
Bloomington, IN 47403
www.iuniverse.com
1-800-Authors (1-800-288-4677)

Because of the dynamic nature of the Internet, any web addresses or links contained in this book may have changed since publication and may no longer be valid. The views expressed in this work are solely those of the author and do not necessarily reflect the views of the publisher, and the publisher hereby disclaims any responsibility for them.

Any people depicted in stock imagery provided by Thinkstock are models, and such images are being used for illustrative purposes only.

Certain stock imagery © Thinkstock.

ISBN: 978-0-595-37809-8 (sc)
ISBN: 978-0-595-82189-1 (e)

Printed in the United States of America

iUniverse rev. date: 8/6/2012

Contents

Introduction

Maria Morales is a wonderful friend, and I will gladly talk to you today about her stories. Maria has led a difficult life and overcome many obstacles. Her perseverance could be considered a lesson to us all. Yet, in spite of it all, you will always find Maria with a smile on her face. Maria's smile warms my heart and I will carry that with me forever. Though her stories are short, they will touch your heart. She speaks of the pain of a mother who struggles to finish her education while raising her family. She speaks of the American dream, and lives by the conviction of trying to make her dream a reality. Maria is a woman who will not soon be forgotten.

The pain that is real for Maria is real for many women across the country struggling to make a better life for them and their children. There are many of us that take for granted our freedom to pursue our dreams. In some countries, women are not allowed to voice their opinions, vote, or go to college. Maria has had a lot to overcome throughout her life. As a wife and mother, she has raised five beautiful children on her own because she divorced her husband. During their union, he was controlling and at times abusive. Yet, Maria stayed true to herself and to her dream of a better life. Part of her dream included attending college. Maria realized that without an education in this country, there was no way that she could live a good life. In this country she found out that with perseverance she would be able to pursue and achieve her goal!

Maria has a message that needs to be read, and even devoured. It is not enough to say that life is unfair. It is not enough to make up excuses of all the reasons not to go to college. Don't worry; the excuses are always going to be there. All of the women I have met in college over the age of twenty-five have had something to overcome. The beauty of college is that you will learn how to overcome these obstacles.

Maria wants to dedicate this book to students and teachers at College of the Canyons. Maria and I graduated from College of the Canyons together on May 20, 2005.

I love you Maria. Never stop believing in your dreams.

Sincerely,
Laurie Epps

America

Visiting my friend's home last year, I was able to see a beautiful picture of her country, Nicaragua. She also has a plaque about her national anthem. I know this is just a demonstration of the love that my friend has for her country. In a conversation one day, she laughed at someone else's garage door that was covered with the American flag. I had to bite my tongue to avoid telling my friend that such a demonstration of love is not something to laugh about, but instead is something to be proud of.

My friend came to this country forty years ago, and sadly she hasn't learned to love America as her home. I came to this country twenty-six years ago, and I love this country as much as the country that I was born in. I was born in Mexico, but I feel adopted by this country.

My children know about Mexico, but they always saw their mother honoring the American flag. One of my children is in the Army, and every holiday I take the American flag out to show my love and admiration for this country.

How I wish that my friend would learn to love America the same way that I do. Sadly, some people will always prefer the country where they were born, not knowing that America is the country that deserves all our love, respect, and admiration. This country not only gives us freedom, but is always trying to help other countries to achieve their freedom. My son is in the Army, serving his country, and as his mother I am so proud of him. I am glad that my children honor and love this country the same way I do. This is my country. This is my home.

An Angel

When I was born the heavens cried
Because they knew they lost an angel.
How to survive without their love?
How to survive without their care?
How to survive in this foreign land?
Not as an angel, but as a fighter.
Fighting for justice, fighting for peace,
Fighting to save the ones nobody will save.
Little children have been my life,
For them the fighter will always fight.
Heavens forgive me. This angel is gone
Because in my fight I have lost my angelic soul.

Cinderella

Like a modern Cinderella, I work from dawn to dusk. My friends are not the birds and the mice. My friends are my newspaper and my computer because they make my life easier. My job is not to clean a house all day long. My job is to take care of a young boy from eleven in the morning until seven in the evening. His parents are the typical working parents of these times. They work long hours to give their beautiful child the best, nothing but the best. I am a modern Cinderella in modern times. The story is the same, but the end is very different.

This Cinderella is not waiting for Prince Charming to marry her and take her to his castle. This Cinderella is attending California State University, Bakersfield, and wants to get her degree in Education. In the middle of the night, my tired body wants to sleep, but my mind starts to drift away as I dream of a new fairy tale. In my fairy tale, I am Cinderella and my castle is a school full of children, singing praises to education and friendship. For now, I only have one student. I feed him and we do homework together, but I know my future is full of students calling me a name I long to hear, "Teacher."

Family

My friend gave me a book. He wanted to share his book with me, so we could have something to talk about the next time we meet at the library. I took the book, but didn't make any promises to read it soon. I am taking my last class at College of the Canyons, as well as two university classes. My nights and weekends are dedicated to my homework because I have to work for a living. That night I opened the book. I just wanted to read the cover, but ended up reading the book for two hours. I started making notes about the book. I find it very hard not to make notes because I am a student. That weekend, I opened the book again, and knew I had to finish it. I forgot about my homework, my dishes, and making dinner.

Something happened on page 192; I had to stop because I couldn't take it anymore. The book opened a wound that I wanted to forget. This book talked about families, and how we are supposed to stick together and help each other because we are family. I lost touch with my family in Mexico, and I haven't called them in five years. Sometimes, I get angry at my grown children because they don't call me, and I realized that I have been doing the same thing to my family in Mexico. I called my friend and told him that I wasn't going to finish the book because it was too painful for me to read. "The book gets better," he said, "just rest today and keep reading it tomorrow." The following day I finished the book.

The name of the book is *"Burro Genius,"* by Victor Villaseñor. I went to the library and asked if they had this book. They didn't have the book, but they said they could request it from another public library. The librarian said that she never heard about it. How very sad because not even the librarian knows about this book. Well, I think that it is impossible for the poor lady to know every single book.

I recommend this book to everyone. This book should be in every Latino home. This book will help people from other cultures to identify with the suffering that Latinos endured in the 1940's. I will always thank Villaseñor for opening my wounds and making me call my family in Mexico. We build fences to divide one country from another. We also build fences in our hearts and divide our families. There is a lot to be said and done in my family, but a call to them is a good start. After all, we are family.

Cesar Chavez an American Hero

The other day, I found a book about Cesar Chavez at my favorite place, the Valencia public library. As a Spanish teacher, I always try to find books in English and Spanish to share with my students. I couldn't finish reading the book without stopping many times to dry my eyes. The suffering that Cesar Chavez went through made me want to write about him.

How is that possible? I never thought that a person who was born in the U. S. could suffer so much. I was born and raised in Mexico, and my father always managed to feed and clothe all of his ten children. Cesar Chavez was born into poverty; he didn't blame his father for the hardships the family endured.

He embraced his religious beliefs, and dedicated his life to improve the lives of farm workers and their families. Cesar believed that they should earn a decent salary, so they wouldn't live in poverty for the rest of their lives. I read the book to one of my students, and I told him that Cesar Chavez' birthday was coming up on March 31st, and his birthday was going to be a holiday. My student told me that he didn't believe the birthday was going to be a holiday because Cesar Chavez was not American. "How can that be?" I thought. "How can it be possible a ten-year old who doesn't know about Cesar Chavez?"

How many people think the same way my student does? I wonder if they think, "Why are we celebrating the birthday of a Mexican citizen?" Cesar Chavez' family left Mexico since the 1800s; however, his last name will always be connected as a Mexican surname.

I learned in school that there is only one race, the human race. Cesar Chavez spoke up against social injustices done to farm workers. Cesar wanted that farm workers be considered as members of the human race, with all the rights and benefits that they deserved. He fought for the poor; for the ones that didn't have a voice. He gave them a voice. Gary Soto wrote an enlightening book about Cesar Chavez. Look for his book at any public library. Cesar Chavez' life should be known by everybody. He is an American hero waiting to be discovered all over again.

Flowers for Mommy

I went to Costco one Saturday morning to buy three things: cheese, milk, and eggs. I was getting the milk when I heard a little voice saying, "Daddy, buy some flowers for mommy." It seems that the father ignored the little girl because she kept saying, "Daddy, buy some flowers for mommy." I grabbed my milk and tried to walk away from them as fast as I could. I didn't want to hear the little voice again. I was afraid that the little voice was going to trigger memories from the past. Too late, I felt my heart aching at the memories of my whole family coming with me to the store. I never made a shopping list; we just picked up things as we walked aisle to aisle. My husband walking by my side, my five children bringing stuff that they insisted they needed. My husband used to look at the flowers and pick some up for me. My husband is gone. My children are grown. Only memories walk with me. I looked at the three things in my basket and hurried to pay for them. I didn't want to cry in public. I didn't want to show my pain to strangers. I couldn't believe that a little voice could have the power to take me back in time, the little voice saying, "Daddy, buy some flowers for mommy."

Friends Ease Worries

"Beside a well, one does not thirst. Beside a sister one does not despair." Nushu (Chinese). The last woman who spoke this Chinese language died last month. For some reason, this saying is always in my mind. I wrote it down on a piece of paper and taped it to my refrigerator. Today, I want to share how this phrase inspires me. Last week, I visited my counselor. She said, "Maria, you only need one more class to graduate." Out of curiosity, I asked her to check how many units I had completed at College of the Canyons. She told me that I have 82 units completed and nine units in progress. By the end of this semester, I will have 91 units completed.

I have six sisters, but all of them are in Mexico. In my years of taking classes at College of the Canyons, I had found nice friends that helped me with my homework and assignments. I am writing today to say "Thank you" to my friends. Thanks for being with me like the sisters that I don't have around me. Marina was a tutor at the tutorial center; she was patient and kind with me, thanks to her I passed Math 070. Maria was in the teaching program last year; she helped me to learn about computers. Thanks to her, I am no longer afraid of computers and I passed my computer class with a B. My friend Chris is taking a geography class with me. She saves my seat all the time and helps me to locate the pages in the book. Another friend is Laurie Epps, I found her last year in my music class. She not only tutored me with music, but she started helping me with other assignments and now we are taking a philosophy class together.

The years of taking classes, working full-time and raising five beautiful children have not been easy, but my friends made my life easier. Yes, "Beside a well, one does not thirst. Beside a sister, one does not despair." Nushu (Chinese).

Friendship

Yesterday, I found that people both young and old have something in common. Children depend on adults to take them places. Elderly people depend on their grown children or loved ones to take them to places. Last April, I took my young friend Ricky to a concert. The Wiggles came to Los Angeles, and I wanted to see them. We both danced and sang while listening to their beautiful music.

The other day, I was telling my dear friend, Caroline, how much I like Julio Iglesias' music. He is coming to Los Angeles for a concert in October, and I wish I could go to see him. My dear friend told me that she was also a Julio Iglesias fan and she would love to go and see him too. "Then it is set." I told her "I will take you to the concert."

My friend said to me in her soft and delicate voice, "Is that right Maria? Will you take me?" "Yes, I will take you." I assured her one more time. My friend is 85 years old, and she has been my friend for the last 12 years.

I enjoy the company of children and elderly people. Children help me go back to my beautiful childhood. Elderly people give me the wisdom I need to face the future. Both groups offer beautiful friendships that bloom every day. They thank me for taking them places. I want to tell them that they are the ones who enrich my life with their friendship.

In my world

Today, I saw a beautiful woman driving a big rig. I was taking my son to work, and I told him how refreshing it was to see a woman working in this field. I went home, but the image of the beautiful woman driving such a big rig gave me the inspiration to write about women.

In my world, I see women graduating from universities at the ratio of 95 to 5. In my world, I see women as Heads of State at the ratio of 98 to 2. In my world, I see women leaving home with a cup of coffee in one hand and the newspaper in the other. In my world, women work 40 to 60 hours a week, then go home to find a handsome man waiting for them. In my world, women are treated like queens, and men never let them do heavy chores like housework. In my world, women are loving creatures, and men look up to them for advice and friendship. In my world, the world belongs to beautiful women. In my world all women are born beautiful, and there are no such things as beauty consultants or diets.

The phone rings; it's my son who needs a ride home.

He asks me, "What have you been doing the whole day?"

"Nothing," I answer, "just the usual: did the laundry, some cooking, and some writing."

I Won't Be There

When I die, don't look for me in the cemetery because I won't be there. Look for me in the laugh of a child because children were my life. Look for me in the beautiful songs we sang together. Look for me in the public library because it was my second home. Look for me while reading a newspaper because for me the newspaper was my best friend. Look for me in a good book, one that will lift your spirits. Look for me at College of the Canyons, where I spent many years of my life trying to get my education. Look for me in the rain and the wind, but please don't look for me in the cemetery because I won't be there.

Letter to Alicia

Dear Alicia, it's your friend Maria writing to you. It has been more than 26 years since the last time we talked. I stopped calling you because I was very ashamed of my economic situation. In our last conversation, you told me that you were working as a teacher. I couldn't tell you that I was leaving the country. I couldn't tell you that I didn't know if I was going to return. I promised to call you another day, and never did. There was nothing to talk about.

You graduated as a teacher, and I was working at a sewing factory all day long. Today, I have good news to tell you Alicia. Today, I started going to California State University, Bakersfield. My golden dream is to become a teacher, and it is becoming a reality. I will graduate in two years. Two years is nothing compared to the 26 years that I have been waiting for this dream to come true.

My dear Alicia, sometimes I wonder if I am ever going to see you again. Sometimes I wonder if you are alive. Alicia, I got married and now my last name is Morales, just like yours. I still remember your name: Alicia Morales Grimaldo. How could I ever forget a name that was called every day in the classroom for three years?

We used to look for each other at recess time. We always talked about the same subjects, always quizzing each other in Geography, Math, or English. There was never a competition between us. When you got first place in the classroom, I was happy for you. When I got second place in the classroom, you made me feel as if I had won first. There was never a competition, just friends helping each other.

I miss my friends, my country, and my language. Only God knows if I am ever going to return. I have a new family and a new life in America. I wish

I could find a way to blend these two cultures together. I know I will never live in Mexico again. I now belong to America, but in my dreams I go back to those happy years of my youth, the years shared with you, Alicia.

Maria

My philosophy teacher told us in his last class that we should try to find ways to get our education without having to work. He said, "Students should write letters to their rich relatives and ask for money." His words made me think, "How about the ones who don't have any rich relatives? How about the ones for whom there is no other way to survive without working? How about the ones that when the father or the mother die, they take on the role of the missing family member?"

That's the case of my friend Maria Martinez. She was sixteen years old when her father died. She was a child herself, and became a caregiver. She came to this country not to go to school, but to work. She worked for five years taking care of her relative's children. She was a child taking care of someone else's children. Education was denied to her. She was happy helping her family. She knew that thanks to her, her mother was able to stay home and take care of her younger siblings. She knew that thanks to her, her siblings were given an education.

One day, Maria started her own family, and dedicated her life to her own children. Now that her own children are grown, she wants to get an education. The education that once was denied to her. Maria is no longer sixteen years old. Thirty years have passed since the day she came to the United States, but you can see her at College of the Canyons taking her English classes. We talk very often about how hard it is to learn a new language. I always advise her not to give up, to keep going and become a teacher.

Yes, it could be beautiful if we all have a rich relative to help us get our education, but sometimes we are not so lucky. We must work very hard to get there. Maria is an example of the hardships we can overcome to get an education. So, to the new students attending College of the Canyons: when you feel like giving up on your classes, when you feel overwhelmed with work, and family life, think about Maria. Think about her struggles, her numerous obstacles, and her determination to become a teacher.

My Graduation

Today was a beautiful day because I graduated from College of the Canyons. Graduating is nothing unusual. Every year, thousands of students graduate. But when you have everything against you and you don't give up, and keep going to school against all odds, then graduation day is a very special day. I know it is hard for regular people to believe that some people are denied the right to an education because they are women, but that was my case. My education was denied to me first by my mother because she didn't believe that girls should go to school. Later in life, my husband forbade me to go to school.

"School has been like paradise for me." At school I always felt so happy. Books have always been my best friends. I recently discovered the reason why I love to read. I was able to go to different places while reading a book. Reading gave me the opportunity to find out about other people. I discovered that there is another world out there, and not only the world that my mother and my husband wanted me to have. I found out that I am able not only to read, but now I can write. In my writings, I give hope to women, I talk about children, and I defend with my pen the right for everyone to have an education. What once was denied to me, today it is achieved. Today, on May 20, 2005, I graduated from College of the Canyons.

My Hands

My small and gentle hands For years crafted someone
Else's outfits.
My small and gentle hands
For years tended mother land And vegetables were cultivated
For someone else's table.
My small and gentle hands For years cleaned someone
Else's homes.
My small and gentle hands
For years took care of someone
Else's children.
My hands have rivers
Crossing them.
My hands have strange spots

Covering them.
My hands move slowly the
Pages of my book, and
Sometimes hold
A pen to write about the Lost, lost years.

My Life

I was born in Matamoros, Tamaulipas, Mexico on March 29, 1956. My mom used to tell me about the reason I was born there. She said that my father was working in the cotton fields of Texas as a *bracero*. Mom wasn't working, but she used to go to the fields to drop off my father's lunch. One day, immigration officers came to the fields, and they took mom and my two little brothers away from my father. My mom was deported to Matamoros, and stayed with a nice family while waiting for my father to come and help her. Mom was pregnant with me, and she was afraid to return to Texas. Father traveled to Matamoros in order to help his family, and in one of those trips, he lost his permit to work as a *bracero* in the cotton fields of Texas. Someone told them about a new city that was hiring a lot of workers for steel factories. My father forgot his dream to make money in the cotton fields of Texas, and moved his little family to Monterrey.

My family moved to Monterrey, Nuevo Leon in 1956. The rest of my siblings were born there, all seven of them. That's why I always call Monterrey my city when people ask me where I am from. I love the city of Monterrey. I remember every single street where I grew up. I remember the friendly neighbors that were just a call away to help us. I grew up in a very Catholic family. Saturdays were the days to do our grocery shopping. Sundays were the days dedicated to go to church, and to stay home doing homework or reading. In those days, it was very normal to have a large family. I guess it was also normal to think that everyone was poor just like us. Traditions were a big part of growing up. All our traditions were related to our religious beliefs. We celebrated Christmas praying the rosary for two weeks before Christmas; we called it "*Las Posadas.*" We never had toys for Christmas. After the rosary, the nuns gave us oranges and peanuts. Up to this day, I can never eat an orange without my peanuts at the side. Another big tradition was Easter. Once again, we had to go to the church and pray the rosary for a week before Easter. We couldn't eat meat the week before Easter. This really wasn't a big sacrifice because we couldn't afford to buy meat every day. Easter day was celebrated by going to church, then going home and eating some nice roast. One day, in 1979, one of my uncles from the state of Michigan came to visit us.

Mother told me that it was time for me to go to the United States and help supporting my family. I couldn't say no to her. I couldn't say no to my siblings. I wanted to help my family get out of poverty, and give my siblings a chance of a better future.

That is my story of how I came to U. S. with a visitor visa, and stayed with my uncle's family. In the year 2000, I became a citizen of the U.S.A. I helped my family in Mexico to survive, and after a few years I started my own family. Two years ago, I told my oldest daughter my desire for a college education.

"We cannot help you Mother," she said, "You have to wait." Wait, how much longer I have to wait to became a teacher and achieve my dream? In 2003, I didn't listen to my daughter, and I started taking full-time college classes. Last week, the counselor at C.O.C. told me that I only needed one more class to graduate. My old country gave me values, religious beliefs, and my traditions. My new country is giving me my education, my freedom, and the economic power to help my family.

My Twins

My twins were so little when they learned the value of money. They used to find the little pennies around the house. I asked them to give me the pennies, not for toys or ice cream, but to buy soup. I still remember their little voices telling me, "Here mom, here are some pennies for the soup." My twins are no longer little; last month was their 23rd birthday. They are young adults living on their own, but they always remember to send Mother some money, so she can cover her bills. They give me money, but they cannot give me their company. For they live very busy lives. One day they are here in California, the next day they are in Florida or Washington taking care of their careers. I wish I could tell them their mother misses them so much, that their mother still hears their adorable voices, offering me the pennies saying, "For the soup mother, for the soup."

Nostalgia

My friend is going to Mexico. I wanted to tell him about the Mexico that I knew. I wanted to tell him about the Mexico that I am afraid to return to, but I held my thoughts, and wished him a nice vacation. He is going to see the Mexico that the government offers to tourists. He is going to see the happy faces of waiters bringing him delicious margaritas. He deserves a vacation, and wants to go to Mexico. I have been away from Mexico for a long, long time. One part of me wants to return, but another wants to forget my sad memories.

I asked one of my coworkers, "How is Mexico these days?" My co-worker went to Mexico last year.

"It's the same" she said, "the poor still very poor, the rich still very rich."

Her words made me think, "Why we have to look for a better life in another country and separate our families? Why we ignore the ones dying crossing the border?"

Sometimes, we try to find answers to the suffering, but the answers never come. The border is like a ghost bringing a nightmare to families torn apart. When a family is divided the chances to be together again are very slim. Some of us live in the U. S. while others live in the land of our ancestors waiting for our return.

I wanted to tell my friend, "Bring me back my Mexico, and bring me back the little piece that my heart is aching to see." But I only said to him, "Have a nice trip and call me when you are back."

One dress, two dresses

A long time ago, I watched a very old movie. The movie was about a poor woman who once was wealthy. She didn't want her friends to find out about her misery, so she tried to hide it from them. The woman was left with only one dress. She wore the dress with sleeves during the daytime, and took them away when she needed to go out in the evening. One day, she lost one of the sleeves, and she cried because her friends were going to find out that she only had one dress.

The other day, I was telling my daughter how lucky I am that my two dresses still fit me after ten years.

My daughter said, "It is not that the dresses fit you mom. They look big on you; you should wear a smaller size."

"I will try to fix my dresses. Maybe a belt will do the trick," I said, to my daughter.

"I can buy you a new dress Mom," my daughter offered.

I never want to have another dress; I want to be remembered as the lady with two dresses. My dresses have been with me during good and bad times. I have worn my dresses to job interviews, to my children's graduations, and to say good-bye to an old friend that is no longer with me. Next week, I am going to a poetry reading because I won a poetry contest. In my poem, I talk about the hardships that I endured.

I will never hide that I once was poor because being poor is not a crime. We just have to find the real treasures in our lives: children, friends, and our loved ones. The director of the poetry department told us that we have to dress formally. No problem, I have two dresses to choose from. The lady from the old movie only had one dress, but I have two dresses.

Placido Domingo

Placido Domingo is one of my favorite singers. Did you know that he not only sings opera, but he is able to sing Mexican music as if he was one of us? He was born in Spain, but educated in Mexico. He started his career in Mexico, and now his music is enjoyed by the entire world.

The other day, I was telling one of my young students that he reminds me of Placido Domingo.

"Who is Placido Domingo?" he asked.

I told him that I wasn't going to tell him, and that it was going to be his homework for the following class. After I left his home, I felt a little guilty about asking him to find this information. I was going to tell him about Placido Domingo in the following class.

I tutor little Tristin twice a week in Spanish. The first time that I met him I asked him, "Why are you taking Spanish classes?"

"I want to learn another language," he said, "and make a lot of money when I grow up."

Tristin is eight years old, and he takes Spanish classes, piano lessons, and practices sports. He is such an eager student, and he is always trying his best at learning Spanish. I know how hard it is to learn another language, so I try to make the lesson enjoyable for him. One of the ways that I'm teaching him is through singing Spanish songs. Tristin not only learns the songs, but he is always asking me to sing them again with him.

I went back to his home today for our lesson, and to my surprise, he handed me a paper about Placido Domingo. Tristin not only read about the singer, he was also able to write a short essay about Domingo. I thanked him because he did the assignment. I told him that I was going to call him from now on "Little Placido Domingo."

My student is happy that he learned about this famous singer. Next week, we are going to start learning Placido Domingo songs.

"I will be able to play the piano, and sing his songs," Tristin said.

This young boy is such an inspiration. What a joy to be able to be a part of his learning process. Tristin will learn Spanish, and he will be able to get the best of the Spanish and English culture just like Placido Domingo.

Romero

According to the lyrics of a children's song, "The world is a rainbow with many kinds of people and when we get together it is such a sight to see." Preschool teachers sing songs to children about love and respect to every human being. In a perfect world, we should live in harmony with nature and with each other. In a perfect world, we are all the same and wars shouldn't exist. But this is not a perfect world, and sadly we kill each other in the name of our differences. History repeats itself in the names of Hidalgo, Pavon, and Romero. They were priests that dedicated their lives to serve the poor.

They were men of the cloth, men of peace, but they couldn't stand in silence over the suffering of their people. Hidalgo and Pavon are Mexican heroes; Romero is an El Salvadorian hero. Hidalgo and Pavon are well known by many people, maybe because historians gave them the recognition that they deserve. Romero is not well known, and that should change because he gave his life to improve the lives of his people.

We all should learn about his life, a life of sacrifice, and love for the poor. Romero once said, "No soldier should obey a law other than the law of God." Romero paid the ultimate price for defending the poor; he was killed while offering Mass to his congregation. Sometimes, we think there is nothing we can do to help. Sometimes we are afraid to help, but if we just spread the word, recognizing these heroes, their sacrifice won't be in vain. If we just let one person know about them, their sacrifice will have a meaning. Romero died for his beloved country, and we should always remember his name. His name doesn't belong to El Salvador; his name belongs to the entire world.

Rules

The young man entered the office. He asked the secretary if he could use the bathroom. The secretary told him that the bathroom was only for customers. The young man left the building. He wasn't a customer. He was a homeless young man. He didn't need a presentation card to let people know that he was homeless. His dirty clothes and long hair did the talking. The secretary was following the rules; she wasn't mean or a bad person, she was just following the rules.

In an imaginary heaven, the young man arrives. The doors are open for him. This will be his home for eternity. The secretary arrives too. The doors are closed for her. She knocks and knocks until an angel comes to talk to her.

"I was a very nice person," she says. "Let me in."

The angel points to a sign by the door. "I am very sorry," he says. "Heaven is only open to those who broke the rules to make life better for another person."

Harriet Tubman must be in heaven. She helped to free more than 300 slaves. I can only imagine the hardships she endured in her quest to help African Americans escape from the chains of slavery. Once she achieved her freedom, she could easily have stayed in her home and enjoyed her freedom. But she didn't. She would return to the slave States over and over to rescue African Americans.

We need rules to live by, but we also need people like Harriet Tubman. She broke the rules in order to help our brothers and sisters. Freedom is something we take for granted. Harriet Tubman represents a fighter who gave her life so others could enjoy a little piece of heaven on earth.

Sacrifices for Education Worthwhile

The other day, the teacher told me, "Today we are losing a student." Her mother was dropping her classes, and Suzie (not her real name) won't be able to come to school anymore." Painful memories about the days when I had to drop my classes came to my mind. In 1989, I took my first class at College of the Canyons. I didn't pass the class. However, I continued taking classes and eventually I began to get better in school.

I remember once, I had to take a final, and didn't have a sitter for my five children. The oldest was seven years old; the youngest was two. I took all of them with me. I went to the tutorial center, and asked if they could stay there while I would be taking my final. A nice lady read them a story. The children were happy and I passed my class. But sometimes, I felt like I had the weight of the world over my shoulders. I had to juggle a family, a job, and my classes.

When the time came, I had to choose between them, and I dropped my classes. There was a fight at home because my husband couldn't understand what was wrong with me. Why did I have to go to school? He thought that I was wasting my time. I didn't take classes for two years. One day, I went to C.O.C. and registered for two classes. I went home and prepared myself for a battle. That evening, I told my husband, "I am going back to school again."

To my surprise, my husband didn't care about my classes. He just said to me,

"It's okay, I guess you really like going to school."

Today, after nine years and forty units, I am still going to school. Now the days are easier. Sometimes, I help my children with their homework; sometimes, they help me with mine. Last week, I started working at the Child

Development Center as a teacher's aide. Just imagine taking off my student parking permit, and replacing it with a staff permit!

I hope that after reading my story, you'll give it more thought before dropping your classes. Yes, it is hard to be a mom, a student, and to keep a job. But please believe me that the rewards when you graduate will be well worth it. Today, more than ever, we need an education. C.O.C. doors are open to all of us. If you must rest, do it, but please come back. I did.

Sacrifices Must Be Made

Thirty years ago, I saw a beautiful blouse in a window shop. I was going home on my bus, and the bus had stopped to pick up some passengers. I thought the blouse cost only 19 *pesos*, so I got off the bus, and walked inside the shop. To my surprise, the blouse price was 119 *pesos*. I looked at my bus leaving the bus stop, and stayed a few more minutes looking at the pretty blouse. Inside my purse, I had 800 *pesos*, enough money to buy the blouse and some new shoes. I couldn't do that; I earned that money working at the factory, sewing many pieces of beautiful fabric. It was ironic, all day long, I sewed beautiful outfits, but I couldn't afford one for myself. The money was mine, but I couldn't spend it. My family needed the money to survive. I left the shop, and walked slowly home.

Today, I went to College of the Canyons bookstore to buy my last book. Yes, it is my last book because I'm going to graduate this semester. I saw some shirts displaying the C.O.C. logo and bought one for me. It's my last semester; I deserve to have something that says that I belong to C.O.C. Thirty years ago, I couldn't afford anything new for me, but thanks to my education I have a good job that lets me provide for my family.

My siblings graduated in Mexico. They are teachers, doctors, and secretaries. I am thirty years late for graduation, but I don't regret it. I know that I played a big role in my siblings' education. I know that I played a big role in my own children's education.

Sometimes, we have to sacrifice our lives so others can graduate. However, it is never too late to go to school and get an education. College of the Canyons will always have a special place in my heart. Some people say, "Dreams come true." I can say that with perseverance, dedication, and a lot of courage, "We can make our dreams come true."

Sunday

An old song says, "There is something in a Sunday that makes the body feel alone." Last week, I had a conversation with a young girl. She was telling me that her family goes to church every Sunday. She also told me that every three months they have mass in Spanish at her church. "My mom makes me go to the Spanish service," she said, "she wants us to support this service or they won't offer it anymore." I told her that I don't go to church, but I still believe in God. She knows that I work every day of the week. She knows that I also go to school, and I am trying to get my teaching credentials. She told me in her sweet voice, "Don't worry Maria, even if you don't go to church, you are blessed." I tried to convince her that I will find time to go to church. Maybe I can go to the Spanish service because it is only every three months.

I couldn't tell my little friend that I am afraid to go back to church. A long time ago, I told God that I will go back to church if he gives me back my husband. My husband is not dead. He is in Mexico, and we are here in America. I stayed here in order to take care of the children, but I don't have little children anymore.

They are young adults, and they don't need a mother anymore. I used to go to church with all my children; I went to church because I wanted to give my children the same religious beliefs that my parents gave me. I am so afraid to go to church by myself. I am so afraid to see those young families together, and think about my family, which now is gone.

I wonder if I need God more than I need my husband. I wonder if God is waiting for me to go back to church, and that's going to be my miracle, finding peace for my aching heart. The old song is forever right, "There is something in a Sunday that makes the body feel alone."

Teachers

Have you ever seen the movie *Stand and Deliver*? This movie is about a teacher who loves and cares about his students. I wish there could be more movies about teachers. Teachers spend their lives trying to make a difference in the lives of their students. Sadly, most teachers will never see their lives on the big screen. Jaime Escalante, the teacher whose life story is seen in *Stand and Deliver* is one of the very few lucky teachers that have been given the recognition that they deserved.

Last November, I had the honor to meet a teacher who reminded me of Jaime Escalante. Her name is Mrs. Dolinsky; she is a teacher at Canyon High. I wish I could be one of her students, but I cannot be one of her students. I am a teacher's aide. I told Mrs. Dolinsky that I like to write short stories, and I need some help with my grammar. "Bring me your stories, I don't mind correcting them." she told me. I started bringing her my stories and she corrected them as she promised. I was embarrassed the first time she corrected one of my stories because I overlooked some mistakes.

She told me, "Maria, you are an artist. When you write, you are creating art and it is very hard for you to stop."

I left her classroom in tears, but my tears were pure joy. "I am an artist," I proudly said to myself.

Her words gave me the courage to keep writing because I know one day I will be able to master this language the same way I master Spanish. I will try to make time after work, and go to Mrs. Dolinsky's classroom to learn more about grammar. She said, "My classroom is always open to everyone who wants to learn." Mrs. Dolinsky is such a wonderful teacher because she genuine cares about her students. I believe all teachers love this wonderful profession and deserve to be recognized with their lives shining on the silver screen.

Thanks

Ana Maria Rabate wrote, *"En vida, hermano en vida."* The translation is: "While you are alive brother, while you are alive." I know this translation doesn't make sense because it is very hard to translate feelings.

Ana Maria was talking about giving praise or thanks to our teachers, friends, or loved ones while they are still alive. But how often do we wait to say those words "Thanks for a job well done," "Thanks for all your help," or "Thanks for believe in me." Professor Lee Corbin died of a heart attack in late January of 2005. He retired from C.O.C. last May after 31 years as a professor of mathematics. I read somewhere that a teacher touches many lives. I wonder how many lives Mr. Corbin touched. I was one of his students back in 1994. I saw the genuine love that Mr. Corbin had for his class. He was always encouraging his students to do their homework, to make flash cards with math equations, and take them wherever they went. I still do that. I make cards for my classes, and use them as my study guide. After I read the story about Mr. Corbin passing away, I couldn't avoid thinking, "He is gone too soon." I meant to write a letter to the editor months ago and thank all my College of the Canyons teachers for a job well done. I am so sorry that one of them won't be able to read about my sincere appreciation to all the wonderful teachers at C.O.C.

Sometimes, life itself gives us a lesson about how short is our life. Don't wait until tomorrow to say "Thanks," do it now. *"En vida, hermano en vida."*

The Wiggles

The Wiggles are a musical group of four silly men dedicated to entertaining children. They are from Australia, and once in a while they come to America to sing and dance for their American fans. I fell in love with this musical group ever since the first time I listened to one of their songs. Their songs are about a fruit salad, a hot potato, and a dinosaur called Dorothy "The Queen of the Roses."

Their songs make children of all ages happy. Last Saturday, two people went to a Wiggles concert. One of them is 49; the other is 5 years old. One of them sang the songs with the Wiggles, the other was eating his candy. I am the one that is 49 years old, but singing with the Wiggles makes me feel like a five-year old. This musical group has the power to lift the spirits of grown-ups and at the same time make young children happy. What a beautiful combination.

As a preschool teacher, I have to listen to children's songs all day long. I have two choices: pretend that I like children's songs or enjoy the songs and sing them with the children under my care. You don't have to be crazy to be a Wiggles fan. You just have to enjoy life and the innocence that this musical group brings to their fans. My name is Maria Morales. I am 49 years old, and I am a Wiggles fan.

Three Questions, Three Lies

He asked her three questions, what's your name? Where do you live? And the always dreadful question; what do you do for a living?

She was only twenty years old, and ashamed of her economic situation. She couldn't tell him the truth, so she lied. She lied like a professional; she lied like the best actress. He was the first guy who ever talked to her. She couldn't tell him her name. "My name is Christine" she said, "I don't work, and I live in that house."

She pointed to a beautiful house. She knew the owner. The owner was an old teacher of hers. He said that the house was very pretty and left, promising to return to see her the following day. She said good-bye, and saw the handsome guy disappear into the dark street.

She started walking slowly, but she didn't go to the pretty house. Her home was two blocks away. It was a very small house full of children, her mother's children. He asked her three questions and she gave him three lies. Forty years later, she still thinks about the handsome guy. Did he ever go to see her? Did he ever wonder why she lied to him?

She still remembers his name, and in the middle of the night calls out his name as a silent prayer. His name was Juan Zamora Aguilar. He was the only guy who ever talked to her, and she had to lie. For she couldn't tell him she had an ugly name, she was poor, and her mother would kill her if she ever found out she had talked to a man. She could never let her mother find out.

Her mother died last year, and her brothers and sisters asked her to move away. Where will she go? This is the only home that she knows. Her hair is gray, she walks very slowly, and her slender figure is gone.

"This is my home," she says.

She was afraid of leaving her mother, and never thought she was going to be the one leaving her. She was a prisoner in this home. She is free now, but she doesn't know what to do with her freedom. She just doesn't know.

To Read and Write

Are you familiar with the question, "What came first, the chicken or the egg?" Therefore, the question above makes me wonder. "What was first, to read or to write?" I started reading at the late age of seven. My mother didn't let me go to school before seven. Actually, she was against me going to school. She used to say that women didn't need an education because we are born knowing everything about children, and taking care of a home.

"You are wasting your time going to school," she often yelled at me, "I need you at home taking care of your brothers and sisters."

However, my mother couldn't make me stay at home because when I found the written word, I found paradise. I didn't listen to her and went to school. I made sure that all my siblings went to school. I feel sorry for one of my sisters. I enrolled her in school when she was only five years old, but I saw the need for schooling in her. Katherine used to cut letters from old newspapers and make words with them. She always bugged me for help. I guess my little sister was following me in my footsteps.

In 1979, I came to this country, and I found out that I couldn't read. I couldn't read because I didn't know English. This was a shock to me. What was I supposed to do? I needed to read my newspaper every day. I went to school in the evenings, and started reading a local newspaper called *The Signal*.

It wasn't easy; sometimes, I had to translate fifty words per night. That's why I always encourage children and adults to go to school, and learn how to read. I read somewhere that we only have to read on the days that we eat.

Yes, the same way that food keeps us healthy, the written word keeps your mind healthy. I invite you to read and write.

Vagabunda

Sometimes I call my daughter *vagabunda*. "What's a *vagabunda*?" she asked. I told her that the translation is a vagabond. Yes, a vagabond is a person who doesn't stay in one place for very long. My daughter is twenty-years old, beautiful, and full of life. She likes to go out with her friends, and stays with them for days or weeks. Then she comes home as if nothing happened. The other day I told her to be careful. "They are going to kill you," I warned her.

"Who is going to kill me, Mom? Everybody loves me."

"Yes," I told her, "I am afraid that because they love you, they will kill you."

"What kind of nonsense is that?" she asked me. It's not nonsense I told her, just remember Veronica Estrada. Veronica Estrada was a beautiful girl, and she was killed a long time ago. She was walking home one dark night, and she never made it home. She was a karate instructor and knew self defense, but she couldn't defend herself from her killer. I don't know if the case was ever solved. I don't know if the killer is still there waiting to attack again.

My daughter laughs at my worries. She has been taking karate lessons for five years, but she is also a very trusting person. She thinks that nothing is going to happen to her. Tonight someone called her at 10:00 PM, and she left to meet her friends. There is nothing I can do to stop her. She is looking for a good time. She is looking for happiness. My beautiful *vagabunda* disappears in the middle of the night, and I pray for her. Sometimes, that's the only thing mothers can do, just pray for a safe return back home.

Without a Home

Today, my boss came home from work and asked his little boy, "Did you have dinner?"

"Yes," he said. "Maria fed me."

"You are such a lucky boy," my boss told him giving him a big hug.

"Thanks, Maria," my boss told me, "thanks for taking care of my son."

I left their home, and went for a walk. It had been a long day, and I needed to walk and breathe fresh air. I headed for the park hoping to find some of my friends.

I didn't find my friends, but I found a lonely young man sitting on a bench. He looked very tired. His clothes were old and dirty, and an old backpack was by his side.

I looked at him, and asked, "Are you homeless?"

"Yes, he said, "I am homeless."

I took from my pocket the only three dollars that I had with me. I handed the money to him, and he gave me a smile and a thank you. I finished my walk, and I went home. I felt a little guilty about having a home, food, and a car. Late at night in the darkness of my room, I prayed for my grown children, for the young boy under my care, and the young man without a home.

My Wish

I only wish these humble stories
Make your heart sing.
For my heart was singing
While I was writing them.
Some stories are happy,
Some stories are sad.
The same way we have sunny days,
The same way we have rainy ones.
In the middle of my suffering,
I found very good friends,
With them, I learned to dream again.
Thanks to my children, thanks to my friends,
Thanks to College of the Canyons.
For my life has been theirs.

About the Author

I was born in Mexico in 1956 and in 1979, I came to America. In the year 2000, I became a citizen. I graduated from College of the Canyons in 2005,and I am attending California State University, Bakersfield. I have five grown children, and work full-time as a child care provider.

www.ingramcontent.com/pod-product-compliance
Lightning Source LLC
Chambersburg PA
CBHW050347290526
45785CB00006B/2668